Essential India Travel Guide

A Must Have Guide for the Westerners

By

Mohan Kapoor

Copyrighted Material

Copyright © 2018 – *Lost River Publishing House*

Email: *Publisher@LostRiver.pub*

All Rights Reserved.

No part of this publication may be reproduced, stored in a retrieval system or transmitted in any form or by any means, electronic, mechanical, photocopying, recording or otherwise without the proper written consent of the copyright holder, except as permitted under Sections 107 & 108 of the 1976 United States Copyright Act, without the prior written permission of the publisher.

Lost River Publishing House publishes its books and guides in a variety of electronic and print formats, Some content that appears in print may not be available in electronic format, and vice versa.

Cover design

M. Abbas

First Edition

INSIDE THIS BOOK

Foreword	5
INTRODUCTION	9
GETTING STARTED	15
FINANCIAL PLANNING	20
GETTING AROUND	24
BEST INDIAN TRAVEL AGENCIES	25
BEST ONLINE TRAVEL PORTALS	26
AIR TRAVEL	27
ROAD TRAVEL	30
A BASIC TRAVEL GUIDE	33
FOR THE FIRST TIMER	33
BEFORE YOU TRAVEL	37
VISA REQUIREMENTS	40
DOCUMENT CHECKLIST	42
HEALTH AND INSURANCE	44
GETTING A LOCAL CONNECTION	47
DOCUMENTS AND PROCESS	48
3 TYPES OF PACKING ESSENTIALS	50
AN INTRODUCTION TO INDIA	53
7 Fascinating Facts About India	53
RELIGIONS IN INDIA	57
SIX INDIAN FESTIVALS	61
RESPECTING INDIAN CULTURE	66
NORTH INDIA	71
DELHI	75

- STAYING IN DELHI 79
- GETTING AROUND 80
- DELHI SIGHTSEEING 82
- 8 MUST TRY FOODS IN DELHI 85
- AGRA 89
- RAJASTHAN 93
- UDAIPUR, JODHPUR, JAISALMER, AND JAIPUR .98
- JAMMU & KASHMIR 106
- SOUTH INDIA 109
- GOA 113
- WEST INDIA 118
- EAST INDIA 123
- WEST BENGAL 128
  - Where to go 130
  - When to go 133
  - Kolkata (Calcutta) 134
  - Where to go 135
  - A Foodie's Heaven 137
  - What's the best time to see Kolkata 137
  - Darjeeling 138
  - Where to go & What to do 140
  - Where to eat 141
  - When to go 143
- CONCLUSION 144

FOREWORD

"If you see India, you have seen the world."

I was born in Bikaner, a small but magnificent city in the middle of Rajasthan, India. We left India for the U.S. when I was 13, and didn't go back till I was 23 again. 10 years is not that long of a break for most immigrant families, but for me it was a huge shock in every sense, especially since I think I left at an early age and didn't go back until I was a grown. The little boy inside me wanted to find everything the way I left them, but that obviously was not the case. I could not even recognize most of my closest relatives.

We traveled to Mumbai (Bombay), Delhi, Kolkata and I wanted to see all of Rajasthan, which we did, then we came back the U.S. and I brought back a lot of great memories along with a promise to myself that I will go back one day and see all of India.

Little did I know, just three years later, I got a job offer from an Indian multinational company that I could not refuse. As I was going through my final interview, I learned that my job would require me to travel extensively throughout India! Needless to say, I was excited, delighted and eager to leave for India.

Long story short, I ended up working fifteen years for that company, but only eight of those years were spent in India.

I will admit that those eight years were the most glorious times of my life, I was mesmerized by the culture, the food the music, religion and the endless colorful festivals that came around every so often.

I always wanted to write about India, and now that I have something I can share, I decided to take the opportunity to write about a simple but useful travel guide that can help people from all walks of life, culture, and country.

To keep this book, short and to the point, I decided not to get too much into the festivals, culture or food other than the most essential parts that I thought all travelers should know.

In this guide, I covered all four corners of this great country, but not every city in every state, because that would be hard to do and the size of this book may go over 1000 pages. Instead, I covered cities and States with most popular and prominent tourist attractions.

Even though I was born in India but since I didn't actually grow up there, it was a steep learning curve for me at first, but at least I knew the language (a bit), and I looked like an Indian which was helpful in my case I am sure. So when I started writing this book, I thought, I can truly bring a unique perspective to this book, because I know the best of both worlds and know how and when to bring them together and when not to.

I hope you will find this book valuable in more ways than one, as not only I discuss what to see in India, but how to get prepared, what to expect, how to plan your trips from a financial point, what type of travel agencies you can trust, what modes of transportations are the best, what food choices are safe.

Let me welcome you to the beautiful land of music, dance and colors we proudly call India; I know you will love visiting here.

Namaste and Welcome!

INTRODUCTION

Rich history, beautiful monuments, culture, and cuisine. India is truly a traveler's paradise. With so many people from diverse backgrounds co – existing in a single place, what more can you expect? I have always said that no trip in this country is ever the same, no matter how many times you go back.

Every state and every city has a story to tell you. Whether you are there to experience the Festival of Colors (Holi) or the Festival of Lights (Diwali), India is a country bursting with experiences waiting to be had.

This book is not only about where you should and can travel in the country but, it's about the pride I feel as an Indian, in sharing the hidden gems that my country has to offer. I like to consider myself a traveler and, having been lucky enough to have experienced the East and the West, but India is an unparalleled experience from the Himalayas to Kanyakumari. No matter where you go, and what you do, you know that you will come home with memories which you will cherish for a long time.

I have traveled extensively throughout the country and, there's nothing that would change my perception of it. It may be a developing country but, it's making progress at a fast rate, and emerging as a strong contender.

It's growing in most sectors of the economy, technology, and innovation. And it has one of the highest tourist rates in the world too. When it comes to tourism in India, there's really no shortage of options. There are beaches to explore, and temples to visit. But, you need to see it to believe it.

There are five main regions when it comes to India. North, South, Central North- East and West. Each of these regions has a different feel. Imagine a journey through the jungles of Madhya Pradesh or a relaxing afternoon by the beaches of Goa. Sounds exciting, doesn't it? And the best part is, the locals are friendly and always ready to help. Because as Indians, Guest is God has always been our motto. And another good part of traveling in India is that most people (if not all) speak English.

To me, travel has always been about mixing with the locals and trying to experience what it's like to be one of them. It's about respecting their culture and adhering to their norms. It's like saying when in Rome, do as the Romans do.

I mean at the end of the day, you don't want to offend them or make yourself feel un-welcome, right? It's not about imposing your culture on foreigners but rather, about being a person who understands how other countries have their own way of functioning.

There are parts of the country where people are slightly more conservative than the metropolitan cities. However, that should not dissuade you from visiting. As in any other country, you do need to be careful about where you go alone. This is not to say that India is an unsafe place but, it's just a precaution which every tourist needs to consider before embarking on their wonderful Indian trip. When you are traveling around India, It's, best that you stay vigilant.

The culture is not limited to the interiors of India. In fact, the bustling metropolitan cities of Bombay and Delhi also have architectural wonders hidden within them. India is a place where you get the best of modern amenities of the west as well as the traditional experiences of the East.

There's a plethora of food, people and learning where you can either choose to be a tourist or, traveler and engage with the locals who would be more than happy to share their culture with you.

For most first timers in India, it may be a culture shock. But, it doesn't take time to get used to it. As you sit in your armchair looking back at your experiences, you know that you wouldn't exchange a single moment for all the money in the world.

As Indians, we are the masters of adjustment and don't want to make people averse to visiting our country. Most hotels whether they're a Marriott or local chain would make ends meet to fulfill a guest request, and that is true Indian hospitality.

India as a country, has a diverse landscape, and you can experience a mountain getaway or a lakeside rendezvous with your loved ones. The roads in India may be bumpy but, a road trip through it is just what one needs to truly appreciate the beauty of it.

From the peaks of the Kanchenjunga to the backwaters of Kerala, India is incredible. It's an experience crafted for the soul and mind. And, as one who's been lucky enough to have been through it, I must admit that my mind is indeed blown.

My objective here is to provide insight about India and why it is such a great place to visit. If you are afraid of going it alone, you don't need to. Many travel operators in India are more than happy to plan weekend getaways and long holidays, and it's far from difficult to get a hold of one.

India is a place where you can hop on a bus and travel all over or simply catch a flight from one city to another. India is extremely well connected and easy to get around whether you want to relax or tour.

For most tourists, India is an affordable destination where one can get most for their money. It's also conveniently located if one is looking to stop over for a few days and there are a number of flights which have connections to major cities.

Planning a trip to India may take time but, if you plan well, then it will be a fulfilling experience in every way. I'd like to conclude by saying, that India is one place which no matter what, will always be close to my heart and mind.

GETTING STARTED

So now that you have a little insight into what you can expect, here's a few things you might want to consider in the planning process. Like I said before, India is a huge country, and it's impossible to see it all in one trip no matter how long you wish to stay.

I will say one thing though, and that is, planning a trip to India is less complicated than it looks. But again, you need to be sure which part of India you want to visit because each region has a different climate, and you want to be appropriately prepared.

This is simply a guide to help you plan, and you may not agree with everything I say but, I'm sure if you do, it'll be a far better experience. What I mean by this is, that Delhi may seem like the historical trip you want to take but, not in May.

Or you might want to visit Kerala however, in the monsoon it will be the wettest saddest experience. What I'm trying to say here is that you need to consider the time you visit, where you visit and what you choose to do. After all, a holiday is about making memories and experiencing a once in a lifetime thing.

Many people are apprehensive before they travel to India and that's common. However, to alleviate your fears, I did a little bit of digging, and I found some useful information which I thought I'd share so you can get the best of your Indian get away. So here they are:

1. Don't Let the Media Dictate Your Decision

In the digital age, we tend to get most of our information and news online. But, most times, it's always tweaked, and sometimes the facts provided may be wrong. A lot of foreigners conceive India as a relatively polluted and unhygienic country. This may be true for the inner areas and remote villages but, metropolitan cities have cleanliness standards, and many cities in India which you will visit are relatively clean.

Many sites also say that India is unsafe for the solo woman traveler. I counter this by saying that this is not true and even if you are traveling alone in the country, you just need to be a little more aware but, it's not unsafe. In fact, it is safer than most other Asian countries.

2. Flexibility Is Important, and So Are Your Expectations

When you are traveling in India, it is much better to have a flexible schedule. Although most highways have good roads and get you to where you want on time, it's always better to account for delays and traffic (because it is a populated country). When you are traveling from one state to another, the routes are long, and you may want to have a rest stop or two on your journey.

A road trip may sound fun but, if you are in a hurry, then air travel is your best option. I've traveled by car, and I will vouch for the scenic beauty that India has to offer. So, therefore, I would recommend taking a train ride as well. When it comes to expectations, India is a mix of simplicity and luxury amalgamated into one beautiful destination. I'm not saying set your expectations low or high, all I'm saying is, there will be things which you may come across which will surprise you.

3. You Will Get Questions

As Indians, we are naturally curious people. We love to learn about other cultures. So, it may be common for you to get a lot of questions. Not only about who you are and what you do, but maybe also about how your culture differs from ours. It gives us an insight as to how we can incorporate some of these practices into ours. I mean, after all, united we stand, right? And if we can pick up some good habits from others then why not?

Another thing I've noticed when I travel around is that people are fascinated with the West and often ask foreign travelers to take selfies with them. Again, not saying that you have to but, it'll just make our day. I mean a holiday is all about meeting new people and learning about them and perhaps making a friend or two you can visit the next time around.

4. Plan Your Trip Around Your Interests

As people, we all have our individual interests. That's what makes travel so much fun. You may be a history buff who wants to explore the streets of Old Delhi. Or you may be a fitness freak who wants to indulge in some rock climbing and hiking. Alternatively, you could also want an escape or a yoga retreat. India has it all.

You can hike to the summit of Annapurna or; you could relax in Kerala and treat yourself to some Ayurvedic massages. And, if you are feeling adventurous enough, maybe venture into rural India. But, you need to be sure about what you want to do in India and plan your trip accordingly. It's not difficult to get around but, some places may not be as well connected as others and may take some advance planning.

You may end up basing yourself in one place and taking day trips from there. But all in all, India is definitely a place worth the visit.

FINANCIAL PLANNING

As you would for any other trip, financial planning and budgeting are extremely important. It's okay to spend a little more than you usually would on a daily basis and, in India most times, you will find yourself doing this. I mean, after all, there is a ton of souvenirs to choose from ranging from clothes to trinkets and food.

I've always found that on all my holidays setting myself a daily budget always helps. India is not that expensive a place and, you can survive a month here on say a budget of 3,000 dollars with food and drink. I would estimate the conversion rate to be around INR 60 for 1 USD. However, it varies from country to country. Here are the latest rates I found:

Indian Rupee	1.00 INR
US Dollar	0.015345
Euro	0.013154
British Pound	0.011633
Australian Dollar	0.020015
Canadian Dollar	0.019450
Singapore Dollar	0.020877
Swiss Franc	0.015280
Malaysian Ringgit	0.064332

Indian Rupee	**1.00 INR**
Japanese Yen	1.742171
Chinese Yuan Renminbi	0.101897

Okay, so the Indian Rupee may not be the strongest currency in the world but, you know you can then get more for your money. Now, when it comes to money exchange, you may either want to get it done from home or do it in India itself. If you plan to do the latter, then my advice is that DO NOT do it at the airport. Because we all know that it is far more expensive. Another thing you need to be careful of is the broker you get your money exchanged from.

So, do it from a viable, trusted source, and you should be fine. However, there are many street vendors who may give you a price which will be too good to be true. Avoid them. I've listed down a few good brokers who you can get your forex done at a reasonable rate.

Here are a few things to keep in mind when buying forex for India:

1. Buy Your Money Before You Travel
2. 30/70 Practice
3. Compare Rates
4. Avoid Traveller's Cheques
5. Keep A Spare Forex Card
6. Make Sure Your Forex Dealer Is RBI Certified
7. Fund Transfer Over Cash Payment
8. Encash Leftover Foreign Currency

As I said, you can either get you forex done beforehand or, go to a broker in India. Some of the trusted brokers are eToro, LiteForex, FXCM, and FBS. You can also get it done from a local bank. However, these forex firms are relatively well known and, have good rates and service.

GETTING AROUND

India has a wide range of transport options. No matter where you want to go and how you can always get there. The two most popular forms of transport here though are road and air. Air travel is obviously quicker and a little more expensive but traveling by road is like going into a different realm altogether.

No two landscapes are the same, and you will be amazed at the scenic beauty a train ride has to offer. It's truly something worth doing when you are India for the first time.

If you are on a more flexible schedule, then internal travel around India need not be planned in advance. In fact, I would just say it makes it more exciting. You can land in Mumbai, Delhi or Hyderabad and then go through a local agent who will be more than happy to assist you with your onward travel.

However, if you are digitally savvy, then booking your trip online is also an option. It just depends on how much time and money you are willing to spend and what you want to explore.

BEST INDIAN TRAVEL AGENCIES

When you are in a country for the first time, it's always better to get some local assistance. You may have an agenda but, a travel agent will just help you organize it better and give you the most for your money.

In India, we have many agencies which plan holidays and day trips. Going through one of them will give you a better idea of how to go about it. Many of these agents will also give package options for various holidays which you can avail of. Some of them are:

1. Expedia
2. Cox And Kings
3. Thomas Cook
4. Yatra
5. Kesari
6. Club Mahindra
7. Make My Trip
8. Go Ibibo

BEST ONLINE TRAVEL PORTALS

If you want to feel independent and be your own travel agent, don't worry. There are many online sites which you can choose from with flights, hotels, trains and such. This is also a more economical option. All you need to have is a good internet connection and a plan, and you are all set! Some of the better ones in my experience are:

1. Travel Guru
2. Cleartrip
3. RedBus
4. Ticketgoose
5. Booking.com

All these companies are relatively well known and trusted. And most times there should not be an issue when it comes to making your booking. They are efficient and have many offers and flights which can get you to wherever you wish to go on a regular schedule.

AIR TRAVEL

Getting to India is easy. Many international airlines have connections to cities like Bombay, Delhi, Hyderabad and even smaller cities like Amritsar. Wherever you fly from, it's easy to get a connection. And for your onward travel, many domestic airlines have connections to get you to your destination. Some of the airlines which you could probably fly are:

1. Emirates
2. Lufthansa
3. Swiss International Airlines
4. Singapore Airlines
5. Thai Airways
6. Malaysia Airlines
7. Qatar Airways
8. Cathay Pacific

If you live on the West Coast, then the Eastern Airlines will probably get you there faster, and you won't have to fly cross-country via Europe which would probably have longer layovers and more flights. There are, of course, many more airlines which you can choose from, and it depends on how much you want to spend on your ticket. But again, you can choose the route which is most convenient and suitable for your needs.

For domestic travel around India, you can choose from a variety of budget airlines. Flights within the country generally do not go beyond a couple of hours, so honestly, it doesn't matter whether you fly business class or economy class. And for the most part, if you want food, you might have to purchase it but again depends on the airline. Some of your options for good domestic airlines could be:

1. Indigo
2. Spicejet
3. GoAir
4. Jet Airways
5. Air India
6. Vistara

Another thing which I may have forgotten to mention is that you don't want to carry overweight baggage to and around India because we all know it can be expensive (even more so than your holiday). The allowance of various airlines differs, and the information is provided on the airline websites. And, if you don't find it there, you can always call the helpline number provided. When traveling domestic, one thing you have to prepare for is long lines and possible delays because sometimes the weather can be erratic.

Indian airports are not too big and are pretty easy to navigate. And should you need help, there's always someone ready to assist you. Since a lot of airlines have many flights, one must be sure to check the counter at which they are dropping off their baggage. Otherwise, it could result in a mix-up.

Self-Check-In counters and online check-ins are also viable options, and I would, in fact, recommend this because then all you have to do is turn up and drop your bags off. For an international flight, one must be at the airport three hours prior and for a domestic two. Check-in counters close 45 minutes before flight departure.

ROAD TRAVEL

Traveling by road in India could mean you either want to take a bus or train. This can be slightly more time consuming and complicated but, it's much cheaper than air. And also, much better food.

I always tell my foreign friends that there's nothing like a cup of tea and a hot plate of fritters on a station platform in India. Train journeys are generally overnight with food included in the ticket price. Frequent stops allow you to experience what the raw, rural countryside has to offer. Always a good photo opportunity.

We generally use trains to travel to smaller cities which cannot be accessed by air. And the best way to do this is to book through the Indian Railway Catering and Tourism Corporation site. Since it requires a login and a lot of information is in Hindi, you may want to ask the person at the counter for help.

Here, I would tell you that if you do want to experience a train ride, book your ticket at least three months in advance to get a confirmed seat. Otherwise, you might end up on the waiting list and will be fined a fair amount if you are caught without a confirmed ticket. Another tip is, always go first or second sleeper air-conditioned class.

Now trains are not as regular as flights, and many trains operate on specific days and times. So definitely check which train goes where you need to and book accordingly. Here are some of the best train rides you can take in India:

1. Deccan Odyssey (Delhi – Mumbai)
2. Saurashtra Mail (Okha – Mumbai)
3. Maharaja Express (Delhi- Jaipur- Delhi)
4. Kashmir Railway (Jammu- Udhampur)
5. Konkan Railway (Ratnagiri – Mangalore)
6. Desert Queen (Jaipur – Jaisalmer)

If you want to experience true luxury with the charm of the British Era, then you can also take one of the luxury trains which are really worth spending a fortune on. It's like a cruise on wheels with the best of food, alcohol, and hospitality. I have personally never been on one, but it is on my bucket list once I have the money. So, should this be on yours as well, you can look into any of these:

1. Maharaja Express
2. Royal Rajasthan On Wheels
3. Palace On Wheels
4. Royal Orient
5. Fairy Queen Express

I will reiterate the fact that train tickets in India are hard to get. But again, we do our best to accommodate people. So, if you land late, don't worry you can always get a ticket last minute from the station as well. (Obviously not for the luxury railways though). Another thing you want to be careful of is the station from which you catch your train since there are many intercity connections all over India.

The information will always be provided on the ticket, and most cab drivers will know which station and platform if you tell them the name of the train. So see? It's not hard.

A BASIC TRAVEL GUIDE

India's beauty is something to be talked about. As you traverse through the greenery of the South to the raw, rugged mountains of the North, it's an opportunity to admire what God has made and blessed us with.

If you are a first timer in India, then you may want to stick to the regular stuff like Delhi, Rajasthan, and Goa. But, if you want to go off the beaten path and really see what we have to offer, then maybe you end up in Uttaranchal or Orissa. No matter what you choose, you'll always be awestruck.

FOR THE FIRST TIMER

Your first time in India has to include the Taj Mahal and Rajasthan. I mean it is a wonder of the world for a reason. And you do not want to miss the backwaters of Kerala either.

I would say take a couple of weeks to see the main sights and then if you have time go ahead and see other things. You may want to see Kashmir and the North East, but it's not that feasible if you want to get an idea of Indian history. So, if you are a newbie, then here's what I would do:

Day 1-3	Arrival in Delhi and rest day
Day 4-6	Explore Delhi by taking a guided tour. Next day, drive to Agra to see the Taj Mahal. After which proceed to Jaipur (The Pink City) and then catch a flight to Cochin.
Day 7-8	Enjoy the sights of Cochin and Periyar which is another gem of India.
Day 9-12	Drive to Kumarakom and take a houseboat ride till Kovalam where you will disembark two days later.

Day 12-14	Here is where you have time to explore anything else you have planned, and this is your chance to take a road trip through India, back to Delhi, where you will catch your flight back home.

This is only a rough guide, and you are free to tweak it however you want. But this is generally the route most first timers take. It covers most of the important parts and gives you a well - rounded insight into what you can expect if you wish to come back. I will be giving more information about various places in India subsequently but, for now, this should suffice in giving you an idea of how you should plan.

From my experience, India can be visited all year round. But the best time is most definitely December – March. This is because the weather is relatively nice, and there's no rain. India is a crowded place, and you will find tourists and locals wherever you go in large numbers. But that should not be a deciding factor. It's like going for the Cherry Blossoms in Japan and expecting the gardens to be empty. You know that is not going to happen.

You need to remember that in some parts of India people also tend to stare. So, you also want to be dressed appropriately. Otherwise, you may also get a dirty look and some comments which will put a damper on your holiday. Not that you need to wear full pant all the time, but when you visit a temple or any tourist site, it's better to wear three fourth pants and a half sleeve t-shirt.

India can also be very noisy with hawkers selling their wares, people doing daily prayers, and just sounds of enjoyment. It's just a part of who we are. I shall be covering travel basics next, and I do hope that it helps.

BEFORE YOU TRAVEL

There is a lot you need to be prepared for when you travel. Especially to India. I mean besides packing, you need a visa and you may also want to get yourself vaccinated before just to prevent any possible calamity. Because being sick on holiday is the last thing you want.

I'm not saying India is infested with the disease, but you just want to be on the safe side. And then you can go wild and eat all the delicious food without a care in the world. In this chapter, I'm going to cover visa and health requirements, Indian norms, getting a local phone connection, travel tips and packing essentials.

All foreign tourists need a visa to get into India which needs to be applied for in advance. I will obviously highlight the process and documents required for it too. If you are a U.K. citizen, then you can also apply for a double entry e-tourist visa valid for 30 days. You can also get information from the official site which I suggest you visit (http://indianvisaonline.gov.in/). This will help you get a few more details too.

Any questions you cannot answer should have an N/A next to it and the best browsers to use are Firefox, Chrome and Internet Explorer. Safari is not compatible with the payment gateway, and one must upload a certain format of their passport scan while submitting documents. If you do intend to stay more than 30 days, then you might have to go through VFS.

For the health requirements, you need to have a 10-year booster for Diphtheria, Polio, and Tetanus. Malaria and Typhoid shots are optional. However, it's generally advised that you get them. You can get this from your doctor, and it should suffice. I will go more into detail about health insurance and what it covers as well. I always say better safe than sorry so getting your shots before you travel is a good idea.

In India, the tap water is not potable so I would recommend sticking to distilled or bottled water. And another thing, if you are visiting for the first time, stick to cooked food. Do not be adventurous and risk your health just to try new things.

Being in touch with our loved ones is important because then they know you are safe and well. So, that's where you want a local connection instead of paying exorbitant rates for your normal phone. Of course, you can get an international sim card, but that is more expensive and complicated.

Generally, most tourists go for a prepaid option, but if you want a postpaid connection, it is also viable. You can go to airport kiosks or local dealers who will be able to give you a sim card and explain the various plans you can use. It's definitely useful in emergencies and rates are not that high.

A good part of the Indian economy depends on the service and travel industry. Not trying to boast but, there is absolutely nothing like Indian hospitality. It's a common practice to go all out and make our guests feel special. Not that we want anything out of it, it just makes us happy.

But a tip or two never goes unnoticed. Whether you are staying in the Marriott or a local guest house, you never need to worry about being taken care of. Sometimes, we may come across as over friendly, but we are working on that too.

When you are packing, carry moisturizer, bug spray, and medicines. Also, your clothes need not include heavy coats and jackets unless you plan to go to the North in winter. You may also want to carry a couple of dry snacks to sustain you during those long road trips. Again, this will be covered shortly.

VISA REQUIREMENTS

All U.S. citizens including officials, require a valid visa and passport to enter India. They have to be granted by the Indian Embassy in your home country, and cannot be secured upon arrival. Currently, visa services are outsourced to Cox and Kings Global Services, and a tourist visa can be for up to a maximum of six months which is rarely extended.

If you wish to travel only for tourism and want to stay for no more than 30 days, then you can get an Electronic Travel Authorization (ETA) four days before your travel date. If you do not have either, you could be deported.

Applying for the correct visa type is also imperative. If you apply for the wrong type of visa then, it cannot be changed upon arrival, and this could result in an issue. Diplomatic visas, however, are still directly accepted by the Consulates and Embassies. If you wish to conduct any religious events, then applying for a missionary visa is recommended.

It is also advised that you carry a photocopy of your passport and visa immigration stamp in case your passport gets lost. Replacing a lost visa can take up to three working days.

Americans who work in designated institutes and technology areas will be required to wait two weeks and also be asked to submit supplementary documents along with their application.

For specifics, the Consulate should be able to assist. People who wish to conduct research, study or any other activity will also be asked to go through the Foreign Regional Registration Office (FRRO) and will be asked to do so within 14 days of arrival in India.

There are offices in Mumbai, Delhi, Kolkata, Chennai and other smaller cities and one can always ask for help in finding the one closest to them. This is mostly done by the local police headquarters, and information can be found on the Ministry of Home Affairs website for its Bureau of Immigration on (http://www.immigrationindia.nic.in).

DOCUMENT CHECKLIST

For a basic visa application, you do not need a ton of documents but, here is a list of the mandatory ones you will need to submit:

1. Completed Visa Form (if you are traveling to a restricted area, then you also need a protected area permit form)
2. Recent Photograph (51mmX51mm) against a white background up to the shoulder with ears visible. (if they do not meet these standards, then the application will most likely be rejected)
3. Valid passport up to 180 days and two blank pages
4. Proof of Residence
5. Dual Passport holders need to apply for their visa on their U.S, passport

So, here's a basic list but, you may want to confirm with an official whether additional documents are required. You can always find more information online as well. And another thing is that for many states within the U.S., there will be different requirements and some may have to procure specific ones which can be found out.

HEALTH AND INSURANCE

While traveling can be fun, one must also be prepared for any mishap which could occur. This is where getting your medical tests and applying for an insurance policy plays a part in planning your vacation. Since we are all differently wired and susceptible to disease, always consult with your GP before getting the required shots.

This is also an opportunity to discuss potential hazards like food, sun exposure, accidents and insect bites. Here is a list of immunizations before you travel to India:

1. **Boosters:** Diphtheria, Hepatitis A, Tetanus, Typhoid
2. **Other Vaccinations:** Cholera, Hepatitis B, Rabies

3. **Yellow Fever Certification:** For India, this can be lengthy, and information can be accessed on the World Health Organization (WHO) website.

Travel insurance can cover a number of things depending on the plan you choose. It's better to take a slightly more expensive plan with more coverage than a cheaper one. There are many plans you can choose from and getting a quote from your insurance agent is your best bet. Insurance generally covers the following items:

1. **Canceled Trips:** this covers the cost of the ticket, tour package and miscellaneous fees you might have paid. There are various reasons you can cancel your trips such as sickness, terrorist attacks, Bankruptcy and insufficient funds.
2. **Medical Emergencies:** Any medical treatment like doctor's visits, x rays, and hospital visits.
3. **Emergency Evacuation:** Sometimes, during an emergency evacuation, insurance also covers the cost of airlifts and getting you to the hospital of your choosing.

4. **Lost Bags and Delayed Flights:** If your flight is delayed or baggage is lost, the insurance policies will have a provision to reimburse you for any expense that you may incur.

Many insurance companies have helplines, and you can always call them if you have a query while traveling. For U.S. citizens, there are trusted companies which provide you with a viable option for this, and they are listed below:

1. Travel Insurance Select
2. InterMedical Insurance
3. WorldMed Insurance
4. Study USA Healthcare
5. High Limit Accident Insurance

Many of these companies might also require you to be a member but, you need not to worry. You can always go through a travel agent who will provide you with an option for insurance included in the package price. So, you can opt for that as well.

Just make sure that it covers the basics. Of course, doing a bit of research into the best insurance policy for you is somethi9ng I would strongly recommend. Other than that, you're ready to go!

GETTING A LOCAL CONNECTION

For many foreigners, getting a local connection can be a lengthy process. But the advantage is that you have a local number and don't have to pay a huge phone bill which will give you a cardiac arrest when you return. You can get it from a local phone dealer but here are some of the best dealers with internet plans:

1. Airtel
2. Reliance
3. Idea
4. Vodafone

Recently, the Indian Association of Tour Operators (IATO) has announced that foreigners who land in Delhi with an e- visa, will get a local sim card from BSNL. Other airports in the country with this provision are also trying to put this into the process to make getting a local connection easier. It will initially be loaded with a credit limit of INR 50 and 50 MB of data, and one can always contact the helpline available in 12 languages.

DOCUMENTS AND PROCESS

If you wish to procure a different sim card, then the process is slightly more complicated but, you will get a more flexible plan. Here is how you can do so:

1. A passport sized photo which should not be scanned and clearly identifiable.
2. Proof of Identity which is a photocopy of the passport with a valid visa stamp.
3. Proof of Address which is the address of a local reference which could also be the tour operator. In case you are not going through one, the address of the hotel you are staying at will suffice.
4. Application Form given by the local phone dealer should also be filled and submitted.

PROCESS

1. The photograph should be pasted in the space provided on the application form and passport, and a visa should be presented for identity verification.
2. The validity of the mobile connection will depend on the following points:
   a. For any foreign tourist, the validity should not exceed the duration of the visa.
   b. The connection will have a validity of a maximum of three months even if the visa exceeds that duration.
   c. A connection for ship personnel will have a validity till the time they are permitted to stay at that port.
3. Once the application is done, then the person will be given some documents with information as well as the receipt.
4. A sim card will be given to the applicant. However, he will not be able to use it before tele – verification. The local dealer will provide this information, and it can take up to 2 days to activate the connection.
5. The tele – verification will ask the applicant who will provide the information given by the dealer,

and then the card will be activated, and he can make calls and send messages.

3 TYPES OF PACKING ESSENTIALS

When you are traveling to India, the one thing you should never do is over pack. This is because you will be travelling to many places and do not want to be bogged down by heavy baggage.

You also want to avoid unwanted attention and pack the appropriate clothes. And in the case of any sickness, you want to be well prepared. During my travels in India, I know that if you are going up north, carry more jeans and half sleeved t-shirts instead of shorts and tanks,

But, if you are traveling to beaches like Goa, then shorts and bikinis could work. I have divided the essentials into a few categories which could make the packing part easier.

1. TRAVEL DOCUMENTS AND LUGGAGE

a. Passport, Tickets, Itinerary, International License (if you want to drive), Vaccination certificates
b. Padlocks for your bags
c. Ziploc bags
d. Backpack
e. Photocopies of important documents
f. Local Currency

2. PERSONAL HEALTH AND EASY SLEEPING

a. First Aid Kit
b. Medicine Kit
c. Jet Lag Tablets
d. Earplugs and Headphones
e. Neck Pillow
f. Eye Mask
g. Personal Care Items
h. Towels
i. Toilet Kit

3. CLOTHING AND ACCESSORIES

a. Thin Trousers
b. Long-Sleeve T-Shirt
c. Half Sleeved T-Shirt
d. Jeans
e. Cardigans or Jackets
f. Innerwear
g. Sleepwear
h. Swimsuit
i. Comfortable Walking Shoes
j. Sunglasses
k. Adaptors
l. Chargers
m. Camera
n. Empty Water Bottle

AN INTRODUCTION TO INDIA

I have more or less covered what you would require before you travel to India. And obviously, there is a wealth of additional information available as well. Anyway, this is basically an introduction on embarking on your great Indian adventure and what you should and should not do when in India.

I'll embellish a little on the religion, festivals, and norms here so that you have a fair idea of how to feel welcome in the country. India is an eclectic mix of religions, festivals, and colors. No matter where you go, there is always something to celebrate.

And if you are lucky, you might also get to watch (and participate in) an Indian wedding procession which is extremely fun. Knowing a little about the country you are going to visit always helps.

7 FASCINATING FACTS ABOUT INDIA

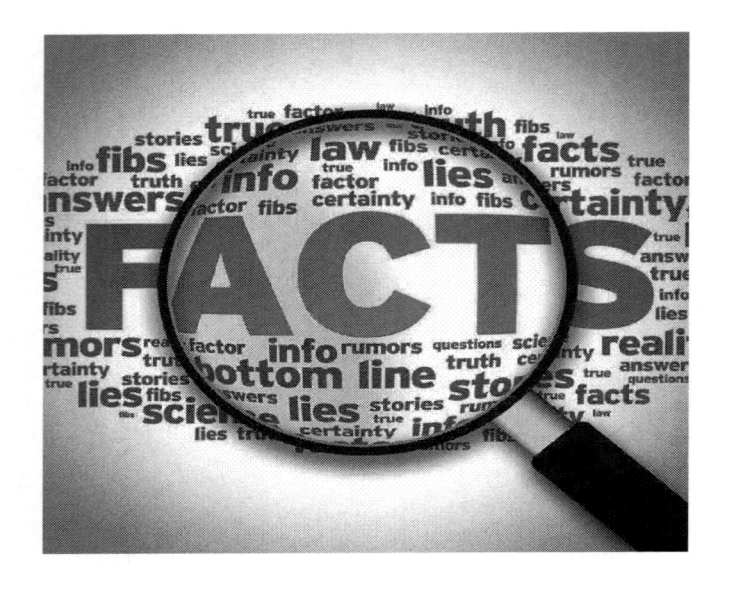

So, if you want to know a little bit more, here are some interesting facts which might catch your interest:

1. India Is the Second Most Populated Country in The World

It is estimated by the United Nations, that India will be the most populated country in the world in just 14 years with 1.45 billion people (that is approximately 1/6th of the world's population). People may perceive this differently as population control is a world problem.

2. India was Once an Island

When dinosaurs roamed the Earth, India was an island. However, once they became extinct, the continental plates collided with what is now Asia and formed the great Himalayan Range. Evidence of this can still be found, and this is why the height of Mount Everest continues to increase slightly every year.

3. India is Multilingual

In India, we are not limited to English and Hindi. In fact, it has the highest linguistic diversity rate in the world. Each state has its own language, and each language has its own dialect. So, in effect, there are over 1000 languages spoken. The most common ones are Hindi, Bengali, Urdu, Marathi, Tamil, and Telugu.

4. Megacities

India is home to three of the world's top megacities. Mumbai, Calcutta, and Delhi. Delhi and its surrounding areas have a total population of about 20 million and are only exceeded by Tokyo. With a large population, many Indian cities face water problems too.

5. Economy

In terms of Gross National Product (GNP) India is one of the poorest countries in the world. However, with a series of five-year plans, the government is working on getting that up. Agriculture still remains one of the largest sectors in the country.

6. Government

India's constitution has many provisions based on the British model as well as those of The United States Constitution. It has State as well as Central Governments. The Government of India Act (1935) is what shapes our laws.

7. Society

India's quality of life ranges from fancy urban cities to rural Indian villages. Most urban cities are similar to the West, and rural villages still conform to a more traditional lifestyle.

RELIGIONS IN INDIA

India is a spiritual country and believes in religion. Although most people in India follow Hinduism, it is a tolerant country and has a number of other ones as well. The only issue with this could be religious violence. But again, it's there in every country. We always say that if you respect one religion let them practice it in peace. Different religions are only various ways of worshipping the same God in your own way. Some of the main Indian religions are:

1. Hinduism

According to a 2011 consensus, it was estimated that 80% of India practices Hinduism. There are various sects of it, and although most of them do believe in idol worship, not all of them do. The sacred books and beliefs come from the Bhagwad Gita, Upanishads and Mahabharat. The 'Om' symbol is of particular significance and stands for auspiciousness. Diwali, Ganesh Chaturti, and Holi are some of the important Hindu festivals.

2. Islam

Muslims comprise if the second largest religious sect in India. Unlike Hindus, they believe in the teachings of Prophet Muhammad and read from the Quran. The two main sub-sects of this religion are Shias and Sunnis, and each one has a different set of beliefs. If they can afford a pilgrimage to Mecca, they try to do so once a year, and this is called Haj. Some important days for Muslims are Eid-ul-Fitra, Eid-Ul–Adha, and Muharram.

3. Sikhism

Sikhs may be a small population as compared to the rest of India but, they are also the people with the largest hearts. Sikhs generally reside in Punjab and the North. Sikhism was founded in the 15th century by Guru Nanak, and he also wrote the Guru Granth Sahib. Sikhs generally visit the Gurduwara and celebrate festivals like Baisakhi. Sikhism is also one of the few religions that do not preach fasting and pilgrimage.

4. Buddhism

Buddhism is a common religion in Far East Asia. However, it still has some followers in India. There is no particular God they worship however they believe in Gautam Buddha who founded it. They are strong advocates of peace and spreading religion through understanding and wisdom instead of violence. They believe in respect and bowing, chanting, and pilgrimage is a large part of their teachings. It also believes in rebirth and past lives much like Hinduism.

5. Jainism

Jainism was founded by Mahavira and is an amalgamation of Hinduism and Buddhism. They believe in non - violence, abstinence, and non-possessiveness. Followers of Jainism do not believe in eating meat or root vegetables at all and can be compared to Vegans. They are also staunch believers of fasting and visiting the temple regularly.

6. Christianity

Christians again, do not make a large part of India and are mainly found in the South in states like Tamil Nadu and Goa. As we all know, they believe in Jesus Christ and read the Holy Bible. There are plenty of Churches for them to worship, and they celebrate festivals like Lent, Christmas and Good Friday.

SIX INDIAN FESTIVALS

When in India, there is always some celebration every week if not every day. And the best part is no matter who you are and which religion you follow, you are always welcome to partake in the festivities. Festivals are a joyous occasion for us to get together, visit our families, and make some delicious festive treats.

From Modaks and Laddoos at Ganesh Chaturthi to biryani at Eid, there's you'll be spoiled for choice. And it also gives us a chance to dress up and put on our Indian clothes which in urban cities we do not do so often. Some of the biggest festivals in India are:

1. Diwali

One of the biggest celebrations in India, this festival is five days long in November. Diwali is a Hindu festival and commemorates the victory of good over evil. In the North, people say it's Lord Ram's victory over Ravana and in the South, it is believed to be Lord Krishna's victory over Naraksura.

People often begin preparations two weeks in advance and since it is known as 'The Festival of Lights.' We burn oil lamps and light up the house. During this period, the Goddess Laxmi is also worshipped in order to pray for financial security and prosperity.

2. Holi

Holi is the 'Festival of Colors,' and it's celebrated in March. It is like the 'La Tomatina' in Spain but, the only difference is that we throw colored powder and water instead of fruit at each other. Personally, it's one of my favorites, and although I have not celebrated in a long time, I think I will take next year. Again, the origins of this vary in different parts but, the crux remains the same. Good wins over evil.

3. Maha Shivratri

This festival celebrates the selflessness of Lord Shiva in order to save the demons from ruling Earth. The story basically tells a tale of how Shiva consumed a vat of potent poison and was saved but resulted in him getting his blue skin color. During this time, people flock to temples, and some also maintain a fast. Drinks like bhang are common, and people celebrate into the wee hours of the morning.

4. Ramadan

Like Lent, Muslims also observe a month-long fast during which they abstain from food during the day. However, at the end of the month, they have a huge feast or what we call 'Iftar' where all the Biryani, Paya, and other delicious food comes out. The date varies, and it is generally announced closer to when they see the moon rise. So, it's dependent on the lunar calendar.

5. Navratri

This a nine-day long festival generally in October. During this time, the Goddess Durga or Laxmi is worshipped, and in the evening people go for functions where there is traditional dancing like the Garba or Dandiya. It is a dance done in a circular motion, which is extremely mesmerizing to watch.

6. Baisakhi

This is the Sikh Harvest Festival and is also the Sikh New Year. There are carnivals and games with traditional food and dresses and events. It's generally celebrated in Punjab, and if you are lucky enough, you might get to celebrate it along with them.

RESPECTING INDIAN CULTURE

People also generally stereotype Indians with child marriage. And this is common in the villages but, in bigger cities, people have a more open-minded outlook. Many Indian households also have a patriarchal mindset where the man is regarded as the head of the family. In this case, women are encouraged to know how to cook, clean and run the house. Again, depends on where you live. Female infanticide is another issue which is why it is illegal for a pregnant woman to find out the gender of her child.

Respect is a huge part of Indian culture. From young ages, we are taught to respect our elders and talking back to them, is a huge no. In more traditional households, it is also common to show respect to your older relatives by touching their feet. We also fold our hands and say 'Namaste.'

A large population of India is vegetarian, and cooking meat inside the house is not permitted. Unless you are in the South, beef is also looked upon as un-auspicious as the cow is considered holy among Hindus. However, in many metropolitan cities, it's not hard to get.

In India, tipping is fairly common in many places. Not that we expect it but, it's just a show of appreciation of the service. So, unless there is a service tax charged, I recommend leaving a tip at any place you intend to eat out at. We also love conversations. So, you might find yourself telling people about yourself and learning a bit about them too. We don't pry but, we're just interested. It's also common for us to do the traditional 'Aarti, Tika, Garland' welcome in many five star hotels.

In many places in the country, we consider feet unclean. But, not as much as footwear which comes into contact with germs and substances on Indian streets. Therefore, in many places of worship, shops, and households, you will be asked to remove your footwear. And of course, this means you need to keep your feet presentable.

You must also keep in mind, that your feet should not come in contact with any religious idols or paintings and be mindful of the position you sit in and avoid showing the soles of your feet.

The Swastika is actually a religious Hindu symbol. Although the Nazis adopted it, it's actually a sign of peace and prosperity. It's a symbol of blessing which priests often mark on children and themselves to signify health. Many visitors find this offensive but, in India, the Swastika has a different meaning, and it means good things. Buddhists also believe that is one of the 32 signs of enlightenment.

Some norms in India may seem strange to foreigners, and one such thing is the right hand vs. left hand. I'm not too sure why this came about but, you have to be careful about it.

For example, when we use the toilet, the mug given is on the left side. The traditional Indian squat is generally how many toilets are designed. When we finish our business, we use our left hands to pour the water and clean ourselves.

When traveling, comfort is key. However, we want to be careful and dress decently and not wear torn or ragged clothes. Indians wear Western clothing too but, you may want to leave your ripped jeans and crop tops at home.

Dressing provocatively can lead to eve- teasing and unnecessary attention. Not that you look like you are going to a party all the time but, you need to be careful.

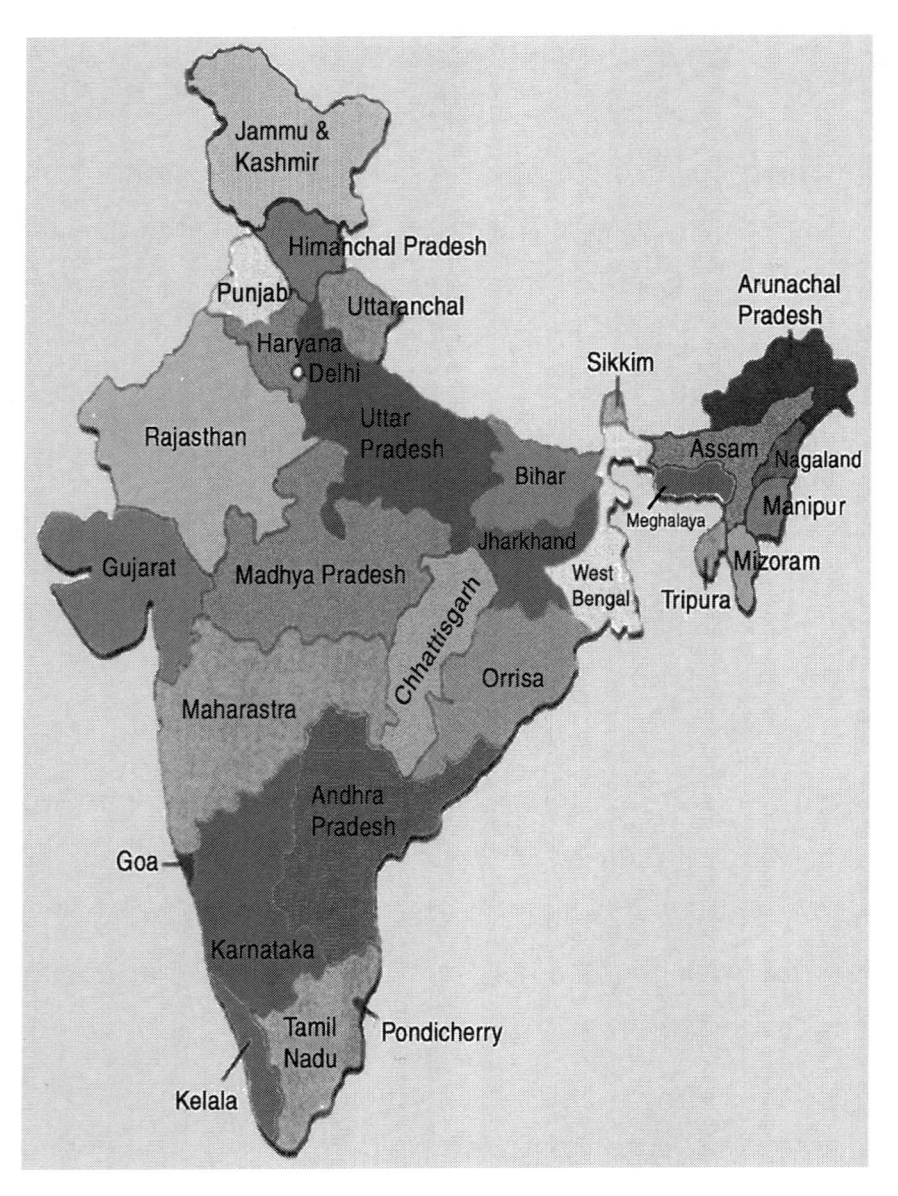

(Map of India)

NORTH INDIA

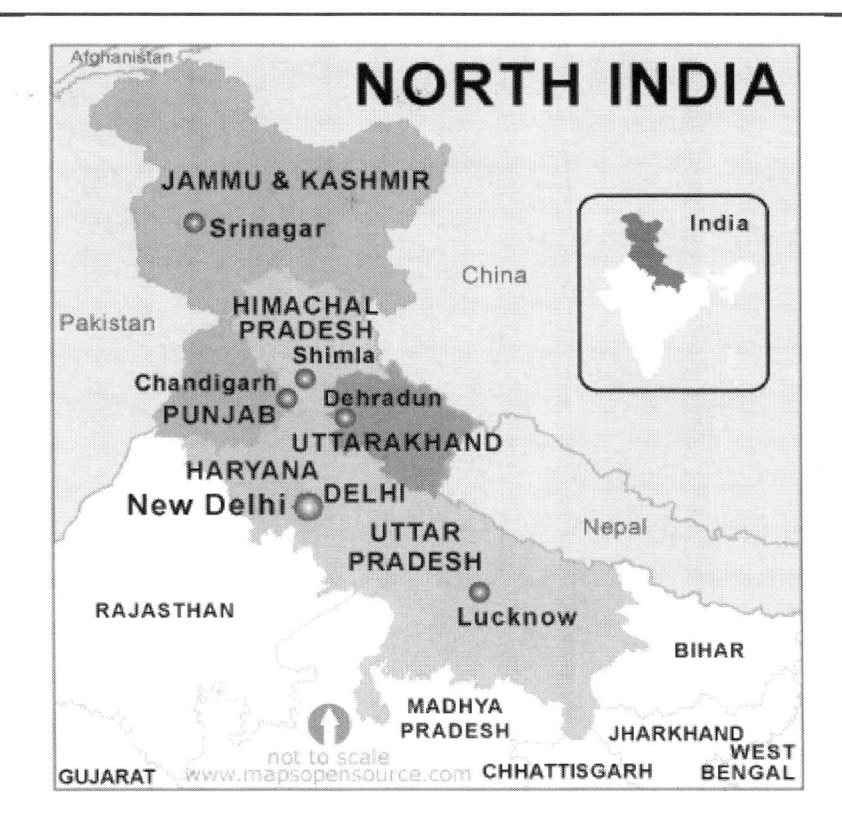

(Courtesy of mapsopensource.com)

When we think of North India, we automatically think if the Taj Mahal. The history of the north ranges from the Mughal and Maurya influence to the British Era. It's truly a historian's playground. Many Hindu pilgrimages also take place up north, and it is home to the Golden Temple in Amritsar.

Apart from this, it is home to the Valley of the Flowers in Uttaranchal Pradesh and many world heritage sites like the Qutab Minar in Delhi. It is the most visited part of India and comprises of Delhi, Rajasthan, Himachal Pradesh, Uttar Pradesh, Uttarakhand, Haryana, and Punjab.

Since it is also one of the only regions which experience winter, November is the best month to visit. The weather is good (maybe a bit on the cold side) but, there is no rain. However, it may be a good idea to check up on which part of it you want to visit and plan accordingly.

If you do want to make a trek up to the Valley of the Flowers, however, June would be your best bet since it is covered in snow for most of the year, and monsoon is not a good time. And if you wish to stick to Delhi and Rajasthan then, you might want to visit in December when the sun is not morbidly hot and humid.

The most popular route taken by first-time tourists is the Golden Triangle which covers Delhi, Jaipur, and

Agra. Some people also make a trip to Jodhpur or Jaisalmer which is home to the Thar Desert. Many times, people base themselves out of Delhi and take day trips but, I suggest taking at least four days outside to visit Rajasthan.

I mean experiencing a desert tent stay is always a good option. And also, you can book a palace turned into a hotel and lived like a Maharaja for a couple of days. Doesn't sound bad, does it?

If winter sports like skiing is more your thing, then I say, go to the Himalayas and visit the hill stations like Shimla, Mussoorie, and Darjeeling. There are many tours which take on tourists who wish to do this. And there, you can rent a cabin or a boutique hotel stay where you get to indulge in authentic North Indian cuisine.

Here is also your chance to visit Jammu and Kashmir which has some of the most scenic views India has to offer. However, you do need to be careful since it is on the border, and there is still some dispute between India and Pakistan over this state.

North Indian cuisine has a fair amount of meat. And if you do not eat butter chicken in Delhi then, you will miss out.

In every state of North India, you will find a different dish to relish like Thukpa in Himachal which is similar to chicken noodle soup. Or you might find meats like yak which in my experience wasn't very good but worth the experience. If you are a tea person, then Darjeeling is the place for you. Because that is where the tea estates lie. It's a relaxing getaway from the hustle and bustle of the city.

When you visit North India, it's a good idea to carry a cardigan or light jacket. After all, it's better to be safe than sorry. Having been up north many times, I must say that it's not for the light-hearted.

From treks in the Himalayas to walking around Delhi, Jodhpur, and Jaipur, you will end up tired at the end of the day but, extremely satisfied. I never knew that India had such rich history until I visited all these places, and I will be happy to tell you all about it too! So, let's get ready to explore.

DELHI

(India Gate in Delhi. Credit commons.wikimedia.org)

New Delhi is the capital of India. It is a lively city which has all the features of an urban city, mixed with traditional architecture. And as you go around the city, you will see how they are so perfectly blended together. Delhi is also where the Indian government has its headquarters. Delhi was declared as an independent state in 1992.

Set on both sides of the Yamuna River, it is divided into two main areas: Old Delhi and New Delhi. It has 11 districts, and many diplomatic headquarters are located in New Delhi. It also borders Haryana and Uttar Pradesh and is about 200m above sea level.

The city was founded by King George V in 1911. It was built and planned by British architects Edward Lutyens and Herbert Baker in 1912. In ancient times, it was the capital for the Pandavas, but during the Mughal rule, Emperor Shah Jahan renamed it Shahajanabad which is presently Old Delhi. The city has been conquered, destroyed and rebuilt a number of times and is home to many monuments such as Qutab Minar, Humayun's Tomb, Purana Killa (Old Fort), Red Fort and Rashtrapati Bhavan (President's House).

Earlier one could enter Delhi from 14 gates. However, only five remain today. Ajmeri Gate (facing Ajmer and Rajasthan), Lahori Gate (facing Lahore and Pakistan), Kashmiri Gate (facing Kashmir), Delhi Gate (road to earlier cities in Delhi) and Turkman Gate (named after Saint Hazrat Shah Turkam).

Delhi is home to many surrounding areas like Faridabad, Noida, and Gurgaon which are huge IT hubs. It is the fifth most populated city in the world.

With the number of flyovers and bridges which provide an easier commute, Delhi is growing at a fast rate. With a tram and metro system in place, Delhi provides a fast commute to its inhabitants.

For those looking for recreation, there are a number of markets and entertainment complexes such as Connaught Place, Lajpat Nagar, Sarojini Nagar, GKII and Chandni Chowk. People in the city speak many languages but, the four main ones are Hindi, English, Urdu, and Punjabi.

Delhi can be a dangerous place if you misbehave and unless you know someone in power, it's best that you adhere to rules and regulations there. Here are some things which might help you survive in the city:

1. Do not use the word 'Bhaiya.' Although this means brother, it is considered offensive, and many people will not like it.
2. Do not crack jokes about the government, religion or anyone in Delhi.

3. Do not get into arguments or fights with anybody.

4. Do not wear tiny shorts and tank tops especially in Old Delhi where you will visit many religious monuments.

5. Metros and trains are regular in Delhi. If you want to avoid being touched in inappropriate areas, then getting onto a crowded metro is not something you should do.

6. Stick to bottled water and cooked food. Even if you wish to have street food, make sure that it's hygienic and always be prepared for 'Delhi Belly.'

7. People in Delhi come across as friendly but, you cannot trust them right away. It's like blindly trusting a stranger who can easily make off with your belongings.

8. If you hire a private driver, you need to be careful especially at night if you step out. It's always helpful if you have a data connection and Google Maps to prevent being taken for a ride.

STAYING IN DELHI

Delhi has a number of luxury hotels with reasonable rates if you book in advance. Of course, whether you get a room in one of these places depends on far ahead you book your stay and season time. Inclusions depend on what plan you choose but, most hotels will have one with breakfast included like in any other hotel. You can book whichever hotel you want within your budget, but I would suggest booking in these:

1. The Leela Palace
2. The Manor
3. The Imperial
4. ITC Maurya
5. Taj Mahal Hotel
6. JW Marriott Aero city

7. Sheraton New Delhi
8. The Claridges
9. The Lalit
10.   Haveli

GETTING AROUND

Delhi is not hard to get around especially with the transport system. You can use public transport like buses and metro or private cabs, autos and even cycle rickshaws. And if you coordinate with your hotel, they will also arrange a pick up for you from the airport. It's easy to find any of these transport modes no matter what time of day unless it's a bus or metro because of those run at specific times.

The metro system is by far the most efficient way of getting around the city. It provides transport to Faridabad, Gurgaon, and Noida as well. It has five regular lines as well as the airport express line. And in every station, no matter where you want to go, you can always navigate your way there.

The metro is functional from 5:30 am- 11:30 pm and has trains every two minutes or so. In peak times, it could be a 10 - minute wait. The metro has an automated ticket system with fares ranging from INR 8- INR 50. (12c-$1). And, the trains are air-conditioned.

The buses in Delhi have also undergone a drastic change. The tickets are computerized, and drivers are trained. There are strict standards for cleanliness and punctuality, and they also run from 5:30 am- 11 pm. Air-conditioned buses are red, and you can find them on many routes.

On an air-conditioned bus rates range from INR 10- INR 25 (12c- 50c), and for a normal bus, the tickets fall between a range of INR 5- INR 15 (10c- 20c).

Taxi cabs and auto rickshaws are common among locals. However, many of them do not go by meter and charge a fixed somewhat unreasonable price. Many of them will also refuse service if they are not heading in the same direction which can be an absolute nightmare.

The general rate is INR 25 (50c) for the first two km and INR 8 (12c) for each subsequent km. From 11 pm- 5 am a premium of 25% is charged. In Delhi, INR 100 should get you to most places. Haggling with your rickshaw driver is recommended as they often charge double especially if you are a foreigner.

We also have provisions to report a problematic rickshaw driver where you just need to contact the Delhi Police or call the helpline ((011) 4240-0400. Alternatively, you can also send an SMS 56767.

DELHI SIGHTSEEING

There are many things to see and do in Delhi. Here are some of them:

1. Red Fort

This is Delhi's most famous monument, located right opposite Chandni Chowk and represents the royal Mughal Empire. Built in 1638, it was intended to keep invaders out of the city. One can also experience the sound and light show held every evening. Entry fee is

INR 500 ($10), and children under the age of 15 get free entry. It is open from sunrise to sunset but closed on Mondays.

2. Jama Masjid

Located close to the Red Fort, Jama Masjid is another marvel of the city. It took 13 years to complete, and the trek to the Southern Tower is well worth the views. When you visit, it is a good idea to wear attire covering your head, legs, and shoulders.

However, you can also rent attire at the mosque. Entry to the mosque is free but, you will need to pay a camera charge of INR 300 ($9) and if you want to climb a minaret, it would be an additional INR 100 ($2). It is open daily. However, it is closed between 12-2 pm for prayers and closes before sunset.

3. Chandni Chowk

This is the heart of Old Delhi and can get extremely crowded given that it is a popular area for shopping and food. Many places offer authentic Indian street food here, and it is a good place to visit to get a feel for the city. Located near the Red Fort and Jama Masjid, it's always bustling with activity.

4. Humayun's Tomb

Built-in 1570 inspired by the Taj Mahal, this is where the second Mughal Emperor Humayun is buried. Set among some of the most attractive gardens, it is one of the first pieces of Mughal architecture in India. A fee of INR 500 ($10) is applicable, and again children under 15 get free entry. Located in New Delhi near Nizamuddin train station, the best views are generally caught in the late afternoon.

5. Qutab Minar

The tallest brick minaret in the world, this was built in 1206 for reasons which are still unknown. Some say it was to signify victory. However, others say it was used as a site for prayers. It has carvings with five distinct stories from the Quran. Again, here a fee of INR 500 ($10) applies and children under 15 get in free. You can find this in Mehrauli South Delhi, and it is open daily from sunrise to sunset.

6. India Gate

This archway in the center of New Delhi was built as a tribute to the Indian soldiers who lost their lives fighting for the British in World War 1. It is always lit up at night and is a good place to enjoy an evening stroll. There is no entry fee, and it is always open, and it is near Rajpath which is close to Connaught Place.

7. Lotus Temple (Bahai)

Shaped like a lotus, this signifies the unity of religion. It is best visited in the evening and is free to get into. The gardens are also a good place for a picnic. It is open from 9 am to sunset and is at Nehru Place South Delhi.

8 MUST TRY FOODS IN DELHI

Food is something which defines Delhi. From succulent kebabs to chole bhature, you can't ever have a bad food experience here. The only thing you need to be careful of is hygiene and spice levels which can give you what we call 'Delhi Belly.' You cannot leave Delhi without eating any of these foods:

1. Paranthas

This flatbread is a breakfast staple in many North Indian households. It comes in many varieties vegetarian and non -vegetarian. The best place to get these is at Paratha Wala Galli in Chandni Chowk.

2. Chaat

This is the best street snack one can find in Delhi. It mainly consists of a crisp base with many toppings like yogurt, chutney and sometimes vegetables. You can also find Delhi's famous fruit chaat which is refreshing and tangy. Some varieties include Daulat Ki Chaat, Bun Tikki, and Golgappa. Any street vendor will tell you that GKII or Chandni Chowk is the best place to eat at.

3. Butter Chicken

This dish originated in the 1950's and is one of the most famous Indian dishes in the world. Available anywhere in Delhi, the best one is at Moti Mahal. It is best enjoyed with naan or plain rice.

4. Kebabs

Kebabs are a variety of marinated meats or vegetables which are mostly grilled. It is one of the best gifts from the Mughal Empire and is enjoyed all over the city. There are many kebab joints in Delhi. However, the best ones are Salim's Kebabs or Ghalib Kebab Corner.

5. Chole Bhature

This is the 'real taste of Delhi.' This dish is popular all over North India and comprises of fried dough with a mixture of chickpeas cooked in a spicy curry. People enjoy this at any time of the day with a glass of cold buttermilk or lassi. You can find this all over, and there is no particular place for the best one.

6. Nihari

This dish is a slow-cooked meat curry (generally mutton). Although it was hard to get in Mughal times, it is now one of the most iconic dishes in Delhi. You can find it at any fancy restaurant or even on the street, and the best way to eat it is with Tandoori Roti.

7. Rolls

A roll is a good option if you want to eat on the go. Although it originated in Kolkata, Kathi Rolls gained major popularity among the masses of Delhi. It is a Roomali Roti stuffed with meat or veggies, green chutney and onions. Every street vendor has his own version, and it is definitely one of the best things you can eat in Delhi.

8. Momos

Similar to the Chinese Dim Sum, these, dough filled packets, are absolutely delicious. If you like spice, then the red chutney is a must. Everyone in Delhi will tell you that Dolma Aunty has the best ones, but again, you can find it anywhere.

AGRA

(Taj Mahal. Credit: wikipedia.org)

Located 200 km (125 miles) from Delhi, Agra can be done as a day trip as well. It is home to many sights including the iconic Taj Mahal which is a UNESCO World Heritage site. It was founded by Sultan Sikander of the Lodhi Dynasty. It is also believed to be the site where the Mahabharata took place.

Initially known as 'Agravana,' it was Ptolemy who renamed it Agra. Agra was also the capital of the Mughal Empire for some time.

People visit Agra for one thing – the Taj Mahal. It is one of the greatest examples of Mughal architecture. Built by Shah Jahan as a tribute to his wife Mumtaz Mahal in the 17th century. It is closed to the public on Fridays, and a ticket to the Taj costs about INR 1000 ($16). To make your experience easier, you can purchase them online too.

The Taj is open from 9 am- 5 pm and sometimes when there is a full moon, it is open at night from 8:30 pm – 12:30 am. There are rules and regulations which you can find information for, online as well.

There are other sights in Agra too like the Agra Fort which was built by Akbar in the 16th century. It is also known as the Red Fort because of the sandstone it is built out of. It contains Moti Mahal (The Pearl Mosque) and Jahangiri Mahal which is also a World Heritage site. Agra is also where the Jami Masjid or Great Mosque is located close to the Taj Mahal. And to the West, in Sikandra, is the tomb of Emperor Akbar.

Agra is a well- known commercial junction and is known for goods like cut stone, leather, and handwoven carpets. A large chunk of the economy relies on tourism, and it is a cultural destination for many. It hosts the Taj Mahautsav which is a 10 - day long festival held in February commemorating arts, crafts and music. About 40km (25 miles) from Agra, lies the town of Fatehpur Sikri which if you have the time, must visit as well.

Another monument worth seeing is the Itimad- Ud – Daulah which is the burial place of Mirza Ghiyas Beg and his family. It was built in the 17th century, and many locals refer to it as the 'Baby Taj.' It is made entirely of marble and boasts of intricate carvings and elaborate architecture. It is surrounded by four minarets, and the intricacy of the carvings of this building can be seen at first view.

If something local is what you are looking for, then you might want to take a walk around Khachpura. It is a small village located on the bank of the Yamuna opposite the Taj Mahal.

In this walking tour, locals are trained as tour guides and take you around and even introduce you to their fellow inhabitants. It's a good way to get a local perspective and how people in the area live their lives. You end up at Mahtab Bagh, which offers dreamy views of the Taj. Again, while visiting any of these monuments, you want to be appropriately dressed.

If you wish to stay the night in Agra, that is also possible, and many hotel chains like Hilton, Oberoi, ITC, and Taj are there. However, I would not say you would need to stay more than one night there. Being close to Delhi, the food here is similar to what you will get there, and there are no specialties as such.

North India is too extensive to write about every destination. However, in the next part, I shall be covering the best of Rajasthan followed by a trip to the Himalayas.

RAJASTHAN

(Credit: commons.wikimedia.org)

Rajasthan (my birth state) has always been associated with the rich Mughal culture, and it is definitely one of the must-visit destinations when you are visiting India for the first time.

With intricately carved 'Havelis,' traditional folk music, stories of the brave Maharajas who fought for their honor and delicious food, who wouldn't want to be here? It's also home to the Thar Desert and cascading sand dunes. Take a camel ride through Jaisalmer or a heritage walk around Jodhpur. The possibilities are endless.

The capital of Rajasthan is Jaipur 'The Pink City,' and the best time to visit is winter time which is October to March where the temperatures vary between 17-27 degrees. It hosts many cultural festivals as well. Its rich heritage speaks for itself, and everywhere you go, has a story of its own.

And in addition to historical tours, nature buffs can take a ride through the forests of Ranthambore and go on a safari in search of the elusive and majestic tiger. It's also famous for its handicrafts and marketplaces where you can walk around and shop a little. Perhaps take a souvenir or two back with you.

Popular destinations in the state include Udaipur, Jaipur, Jaisalmer, Jodhpur, Pushkar and Mount Abu, Ranthambore, and Bikaner (this is where I was born). This may seem like a lot of places to visit, but believe me that this is only the tip of the iceberg.

(Anup Mahal in Bikaner. Credit: Wikipedia.org)

If you are looking for a royal experience, then you are in the right place. Rajasthan echoes the true spirit of heroism and bravery and many Indian war poems about the Rajputs reflect the fact that it is overflowing with history, yet has all the elements of modern times.

Rajasthan originated as the region of Rajputana, shortly after the Gupta Era ended. This being a coveted area, was the site of many bloody wars and battles between the Rajputs and other empires, mainly the Mughals.

The Rajputs ruled the region for a relatively long time until the beginning of the British Rule in India, which we all know lasted two centuries. As India gained independence, Rajasthan which initially comprised of 18 provinces, was merged into one state and Maharaja of Jaipur was given the absolute power of governance.

Rajasthan's landscape is diverse and well divided by the Aravali Range from Northwest to Southeast. Agricultural land is mainly in the East. It is also home to the Thar Desert which boasts of beautiful cascading sand dunes, and the Chambal River which is the only source of water in the state.

Pushkar is one of the oldest cities in Rajasthan. Situated at the height of 510 meters above sea level, it is surrounded by hills on three sides and is located to the North West of Ajmer. The 'Nag Pahad' or Snake Mountain, is the hill which separates the two cities.

According to mythology, it was Lord Brahma who created the city of Pushkar, and it is considered a pilgrimage place for many Hindus who believe you need to do it at least once in your life to attain salvation. The Pushkar Lake is considered as holy as the Ganges, and no pilgrimage is complete without a dip in the lake.

The Brahma Temple, which is the only temple in India dedicated to Lord Brahma, is near Snake Mountain. Built with marble and decorated with coins, it can be identified from its red spire and an image of a swan which Lord Brahma considered sacred.

The inner sanctum has many idols of Gods, but the main attraction is obviously the one of Lord Brahma. In addition to this temple, there are many more which you can visit as well, but otherwise, it's more of a holy place which can be covered in a day trip if you are staying in Jaipur.

In many parts of Rajasthan, you can get there by train or road, and it is not difficult to get from one place to another. But, since train tickets are a little difficult to get at the last minute, your best bet would be either renting a car, taking a bus or even flights depending on how much time you want to spend in each place.

If you do have time, then you must also visit Mount Abu, Bikaner or Ranthambore which all beautiful in their own way. If you do want to read more on Rajasthan in detail, you can visit the Rajasthan Tourism site for which the link is (http://tourism.rajasthan.gov.in)

UDAIPUR, JODHPUR, JAISALMER, AND JAIPUR

(Hawa Mahal in Jaipur. Credit: commons.wikimedia.org)

Udaipur is one of the most iconic cities in Rajasthan and is known as 'The Venice of the East.' Surrounded by lakes and lush green mountains, it is also known as 'The City of Lakes.' The Lake Palace, situated in the middle of Pichola Lake, is truly a sight to behold. Jaisamand Lake is believed to be the largest sweet water man-made a lake in Asia and is also worth a visit. Adding to the charm of the city is the City Palace and Monsoon Palace which emulate the architectural grandeur of the Rajputs.

The Solar Observatory, based on the Big Bear Lake model, is the only observatory in India located on an island.

There is much to see and do in Udaipur, and it is impossible to list all the sights in one go. However, some of them include The Ahar Museum, where you can find Rajout artifacts and pottery, and Jagdish Temple which is a place of worship dedicated to the Indian God Vishnu.

Saheliyon Ki Bari and Gulab Bagh are also popular tourist sites which are palaces which have been converted to museums boasting of magnificent gardens. If you like nature, then a visit to Udaipur Biological Park is an absolute must visit. It aims to conserve the endangered species in the area and the best time to visit the Park is between July-September.

Jodhpur is also known as the 'Blue City' and is the second largest city in Rajasthan. Forts, palaces, and houses are all built in vibrant shades of blue from which the city gets its name. The towering fort of Mehrangarh is where the old city was originally located, and the new city is outside the gates of this fort.

Jodhpur is also known for its breed of horses called Malani or Marwari horses which are only found here. The city was built in 1459 AD by the Rathore clan and was the capital of the state of Marwar. Hence people from Jodhpur are also called Marwaris.

Mehrangarh Fort is one of the definite must visits while in Jodhpur. Towering 125 meters above the city, it is known for its exquisite window carvings, and Phool Mahal (Flower Palace), Moti Mahal (Pearl Palace), and Sheesh Mahal (Crystal Palace).

Khejarla Fort is a little drive away but, it is definitely worth the journey. It is only one of the many Rajput forts which are a part of the state. Umaid Bhavan Palace was initially built as a shelter when famine struck the state in 1929. Now, a grand palace, it was built in an Indo- Western style with art deco elements too.

Moti Mahal or 'The Pearl Palace' was where the kings held their audience. It is said to have five nooks through which the queen could hear the ongoing discussions. Sheesh, Mahal and Phool Mahal are again two halls which are part of Mehrangarh Fort, with carvings of religious figures and intricate designs.

Besides all of these, one can also visit Balsanda Lake, Guda Village, Somnath Temple, Ghanta Ghar (The Bell House) and other sights of interest. Of course, one has to plan accordingly, but Udaipur and Jodhpur are two cities one will have to keep revisiting to soak in everything.

And let me say that, you will keep coming back – for the food if nothing else! In terms of history culture and food, there is truly nothing like Rajasthan!

When it comes to traveling around, car and road is your best bet. But again, we'll get to that part in a bit. One must also note that Rajasthan is predominantly vegetarian since it is where Marwaris are from. But again, there is no dearth of non - vegetarian options for those who like a little meat.

Jaisalmer is a geologist's paradise with a fossil park just 15 km away from the city. Also known as 'The Golden City,' it acts as a gate to the rest of North India and that is where the greatest Thar Desert begins. Jaisalmer's Golden Fort is not simply a tourist attraction, rather a complex of shops, homes, and hotels for which generations have been living in forever.

Jaisalmer gets its name from Rawal Jaisal who set out in search of a capital city for his kingdom. He came across a town called Eesul and built a mud fort and renamed it Jaisalmer. There are many things to see and do in Jaisalmer, one of the most popular being the desert festival. This is hosted in January and February with a host of activities like camel races, puppet shows, folk dances and a lot more.

The best way to tour Jaisalmer is to walk around the city or take a taxi to various attractions. Besides Sonar Killa (The Gold Fort) there is Nathmal, Salim and Patwon's Haveli which were all built to celebrate the architectural style of the Rajputs. Hence, it comes as no surprise that these have intricate carvings and boast of great architecture.

The more you explore the city, the more you will fall in love with it. The Cloud Palace is a five stories structure with a carved balcony is the art of Muslim architects and offers great views of the city. Gadisar Lake is a pilgrimage center and a human-made lake built in the 14th century.

Jaipur was the first planned city in India. Famous for its gems, the city is known to mix culture and modernism. It is part of what we call the 'Golden Triangle' which includes Delhi and Agra as well. Jaipur is also called the Pink City because the town was painted pink in honor of the Prince of Wales.

The city was the capital of Jai Singh II when he shifted here from Amber due to the scarcity of water. Amber Palace and the City Palace are two of the must-see in the city. Both were built as citadels and are located a little bit out of the city. In the City Palace, one can find royal costumes and play dress up and also find world-famous Pashmina shawls.

Jantar Mantar is a UNESCO World Heritage site which is one of the oldest and largest observatories in the world. It has many activities and tools which allow tourists to learn about chronology and other aspects of astronomy.

Hawa Mahal or The Wind Palace is where the royal ladies used to observe the happenings in the city without being seen themselves. It is a five-storied structure and is a mix of Hindu and Muslim architecture. The most prominent feature is the latticed windows which are known as Jharokas. If you are feeling adventurous, then climb up and get a view of the city.

JAMMU & KASHMIR

(Mughal Garden in Srinagar, Kashmir. Credit: Wikipedia.org)

Jammu and Kashmir may be the center of conflict between India and Pakistan, but that does not stop it from being one of the most picturesque places in India. Located between The Himalayas and the Pir Panjal ranges, this is one place which should be on your bucket list if it isn't already. It's also the state which is the source for many rivers in India with foliage, greenery, and lakes surrounding it.

The Mughals aptly named this place 'Paradise on Earth', and when you visit it, you will know why. The Mughals left behind a legacy with palaces and gardens, as well as their style of arts and crafts which have been passed down through many generations. The snow - clad mountains, make for a great winter getaway where you can go skiing, and sled riding as well as many other activities.

Barring Himachal Pradesh, Jammu & Kashmir is probably the only place in India with four distinct seasons – spring, summer, autumn, and winter. Each season has a character of its own and no matter when you wish to visit, beauty will surround you from every side. Spring is the best season to visit and extends from March to May. If you are lucky, the temperature will be 23 degrees, or it can also get cold and drop to 6 degrees. Either way, you must carry warm clothes.

You might also experience rainy weather, but the showers are not very heavy. From June to August, it is summertime. And here is where you will see myriad shades of green all over. The temperature generally does not go above 35 degrees, and it is a refreshing change from the unbearable heat.

From September to December, it's autumn. And this is where India experiences fall. The leaves are shades of rust, yellow and red and it is a sight to behold. Temperatures drop by this time to 10 degrees, and if you are visiting, heavy woolens must be carried, or you might freeze to death.

If you have never experienced snowfall, then December is the time to visit where the White Mountains tower over the valleys. There are very few hotels which are open but, most of them are centrally heated, and you do not need to worry about keeping warm.

SOUTH INDIA

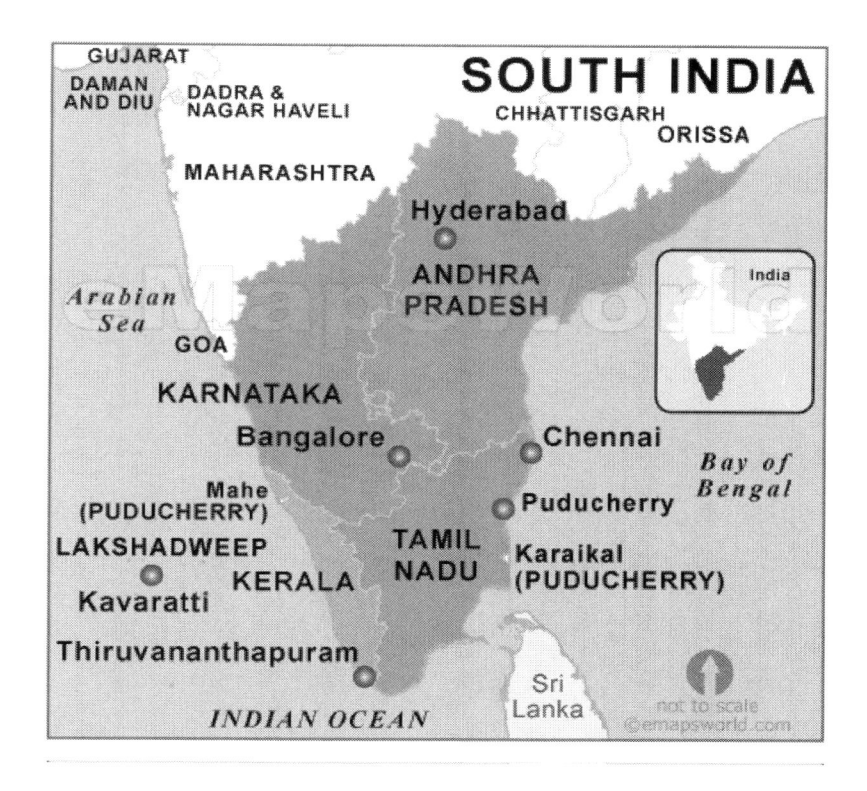

(Credit: mapsopensource.com)

South India is known for its myriad temples and amalgamation of cultures. It has a diverse history and has been the capital of many dynasties in the past. It is definitely one of the more religious parts of the country, and hence people are more conservative. But that's not to say it is not fun. For example, the state of Goa is known as the 'Party State' of the country and is frequented by visitors all year round.

There are eight states in total. Kerala, Andhra Pradesh, Tamil Nadu and Karnataka are the most visited because they also have the best connectivity. There are flights to Chennai, Bangalore, and Cochin and you can get some good deals if you book in advance.

Tamil Nadu is known as 'The Land of The Temples.' It's known for its beauty and magnificent temples. Chennai is the capital of the state and is the gateway to Tamil Nadu. It is also the state which gets the maximum foreign investments like automobiles, IT, power and telecommunication. Along with temples, it also has many wildlife sanctuaries for all you outdoor buffs who enjoy a safari.

The beaches are also fast becoming a huge tourist attraction. Marina Beach is the second longest in the world, and Elliott Beach is also a popular shopping destination. Long Beach, Kanyakumari Beach and

Mahabalipuram Beach are also must-visits if you are in the area and have time.

Kerala is better known as God's Own Country, and when you visit, you will come to know why. It has the highest literacy rate in India, and Ayurveda originates from this state. The climate is cool, and the monsoon is the best time to visit which is from June-September.

The seafood is to die for, and there are many ways of preparing fish which come fresh from the sea almost every morning. The backwaters are a must do when in Kerala as they make for a relaxing getaway and are a beautiful way to explore the state. Many people book their tours when they arrive in Kerala, and it is not hard to find. However, an advance booking is recommended.

Karnataka is another hidden gem in which the capital city of Bangalore is a must visit. With food and culture, this should definitely be on your bucket list. The numerous forts, temples, and mosques make it a land of diversity and a state worth exploring.

If temples are something that interests you, then you must visit Hampi which is the oldest preserved temple complex in India. The jungles of Karnataka make for the perfect wildlife getaway too. It is said that many great writers came here to write their books and it is one of the states in India which has that hidden charm.

Andhra Pradesh is one of the most fertile states and is surrounded by rivers and mountains. Its main industry is agriculture given that the soil is extremely fertile and good for crop growing. Although it may not have a great climate and can get very hot in the summer, winter is the time to visit this place. Vishakhapatnam is India's fourth largest port and is located here.

It is also a state of religious interests and Hyderabad, has some of the best biryani in the country and is famous all over. It's also well known for education, and many prestigious universities are located here. To know more about South India tourism, do visit (https://www.southtourism.in/andrapradesh)

GOA

(Arambol Beach in Goa Credit: wikipedia.org)

We now get to the state of Goa, where the beaches are beautiful, food is great and people friendly. Known as the party state of India, once you visit this place, you will know why. That's not to say it does not have a history because the Portuguese influence from homes to churches can be seen all over and it is a hippie's paradise.

If you are a beach lover, then this is definitely the state to visit because all you need to do is get your bikini on and relax by the sea as you sip on a cold one! Goa, as they say, is a feeling and once you have seen the place, it's not hard to see.

You can reach Goa by air, rail or road. The International Airport (Dabolim) is well connected, and you can get there from many metropolitan cities like Mumbai, Bangalore, and Delhi. By train, you can get off in Pernem, Thivim or Canacona and get to Panjim where you can get local transport to the inner part of the state. The best way, however, is a self-driven car or a rental car (with driver) to do this as it is much safer than buses and public transport.

This is the smallest state in India and going from one side to another does not take much time. Where you want to stay depends on what your agenda is, and South Goa is known for its pristine beaches. North Goa, on the other hand, is known for the party scene and nightclubs.

There are many economical options when it comes to hotels, and the best deals can be found online on sites like TripAdvisor or MakeMyTrip.com. If you like shopping, then this is also the place for you because you get so many local artifacts, that it is hard to choose.

However, one must be able to bargain as well as people may quote a price higher than its value, and you might want to check the quality at times too. If you are a big group, then Airbnb has good deals on villas and homestays where you can have a private getaway with your friends and enjoy the state at your own pace.

Some of the most popular beaches in Goa are Calangute, Baga, Anjuna and Morjim Beach. A good way to enjoy this beach culture is to go to the shacks which are open all summer long and enjoy their seafood preparations like squid, crab, kingfish and pomplet fish.

The seafood is fresh, and one of the best things to eat in Goa is their beef chili fry and Continental food. Of course, there's no shortage of options, but Martins Corner is one of the most famous joints in Goa for their specialty Prawn Recheado, and you cannot leave Goa without giving it a try. It's all about food friends and good times here.

Exploring the state with its forts and churches in Old Goa is something very interesting you can do. You'll learn about the history and facts and get to learn that it has much more to it than meets the eye. St Peter's Cathedral is one of the most famous ones and contains the remains of St Peter who was a prominent figure. It's worth exploring, and many tours take you around the city where you can learn, shop and eat.

If you are visiting Goa in the monsoon (which I would advise against), it's always better to be prepared with raingear and appropriate shoes. But again, it's no fun as all the shacks are closed, and there are far fewer options to enjoy. Goa is lively all year round, and it is easy to make friends.

It is also one of the states where one can walk and drink because alcohol is easily available in many shops. Alcohol here does not have taxes, and henceforth it's also affordable.

WEST INDIA

(Credit: mapsopensource.com & emapsworld.com)

West India is the region which contains Maharashtra, Gujarat and Daman and Diu. Other people may also argue that Goa and Rajasthan are part of this.

However, it was always a debatable topic. Marathi, Gujarati, and Rajasthani are the widely spoken languages of this region, and it has much to explore and see. Famous cities include Mumbai, Pune, Nasik, Gandhinagar, Ahmedabad and hill stations like Matheran and Mahabaleshwar.

A lot of these cities have a largely urban population as they are big and Mumbai is known as the land of opportunity since that is where the Bollywood industry is as well.

There are many places one can visit, and Dadra and Nagar Haveli is famous for its rolling hills, greenery, and wildlife. Situated in the Western Ghats. Some famous places you can visit here are the Tribal Garden in Silvassa, Vanganga Lake, and Hirawan Garden. Daman and Diu are known for its tranquility amidst marshlands and limestone cliffs.

The state also has beautiful beaches, churches, and gardens. Gujarat is the state where Mahatma Gandhi is from, and it has many educational institutes where people come from far and wide to learn. Maharashtra houses the great city of Mumbai which is the financial capital of the country,

The best time to visit this region is in winter which is from November- March. The summer in all of these states can get excruciatingly hot, and the travel experience is beautiful but not pleasant. Indian festivals like Navratri and Ganesh Chaturthi are celebrated widely in this region, and the cuisine is a lot of seafood, kokum, nuts and Gujarati cuisine is predominantly vegetarian.

Many tourists also make day trips like that to Elephanta Caves and Alibagh which are popular weekend getaways for the locals here. It is important to plan carefully as you do not want to be running around all over.

There is a lot to see and do around these states, and I will highlight a few things to do as well. However, there is no dearth of activity you can choose from by yourself as well. If it's hiking you want, then you can go to the Sahyadris and Mount Abu. If it's a beach holiday, then Goa and Ganpatiphule are good options.

The culture varies from state to state, and you will be able to see how people live in and around these areas. Getting around here can be done mainly by road or rail, and of course, there are airports which connect to the major cities as well if you like shorter travel time.

Parts of Western India were also part of the Indus Valley Civilization and sites uncovered include Lothal and Surkotada. Western India has seen many dynasties from the Rajputs, to the Mughals and Marathas. It then, of course, came under the British Colonial Rule and after a long 200- year struggle, gained independence in 1947.

The region is accountable for about 24% of the country's GDP as well. This is also a relatively safe part of the country where the crime rate is low, but of course in big cities, it is important to keep track of your important belongings as Mumbai and Pune may have a few pickpockets.

One thing you must keep in mind is that Gujarat is the only dry state in India where you cannot purchase alcohol without a special permit. However, in Daman and Diu, the taxes are low on alcohol and is popular getaway for the locals of the state when they want a drink or two.

Drinking on the street in any of these states can be offensive to the locals, and one must refrain from doing so. However, all said, it's an easy- going area except of course for the large cities where everything is in chaos, but you learn to love.

EAST INDIA

(Credit: mapsopensource.com)

East India contains the states of West Bengal, Nagaland, Mizoram, Manipur, Tripura, Arunachal Pradesh, Assam, and Meghalaya. Sometimes, people also say that Sikkim comes under this, but again that is a debatable point. These are also known as the seven sisters, and they are unexplored slices of paradise with beautiful vistas and unbelievable scenery.

This part of the country is also known for its tribal culture and spicy food. If you want a quiet holiday, then the Northeast is the place to visit because the only thing around you is the majestic mountains and lush greenery.

The Northeast is also where sustainable tourism happens, and many areas were restricted to foreigners until very recently. Arunachal Pradesh's proximity to China has seen many restrictions and people who wish to visit require a special permit to do so.

Although it has become slightly more relaxed, this is not a place where one should travel alone. Many adventurous Indians flock to Tawang to visit India's largest monastery which houses a number of Tibetan paintings. And the Torgya festival in January as well as the Tawang Festival in October. The Ziro Music Festival is also celebrated here and is held in late

September and is a popular festival attended by locals and tourists alike.

Assam is where about 60% of India's tea is grown and is famous the world over. It is the most accessible of all Northeast Indian states where you can start your journey into the great Northeast. Guwahati is said to be rather unattractive, but many people tend to stay there a few days and base themselves out of here since it is fairly accessible and easy to get to.

The most visited place is Assam is Kaziranga National Park which is home to the one-horned Rhinoceros. However, there is no shortage of wildlife parks here. One must also visit Majuli which is the world's largest inhabited river island.

Nagaland is the land of tribes, and there are about 16 known tribes here. Locals are friendly, and many tourist lodges have cultural programs where the locals come and perform dances, songs and entertain them.

Two major festivals, the Hornbill (December) and Moatsu (May) are really what has placed this humble state on the tourist map. Manipur is the farthest state in India bordering Bangladesh and Burma and is known for its lakes, mountains and swampy land. Loktak Lake is said to be the only floating lake in the world and is worth a visit. Sendra Park and Resort is the best place to stay in order to experience this.

Meghalaya is the Abode of the clouds as it is one of the wettest places on earth. Sop choosing your time to visit here should be done wisely, and it is unsafe to visit during monsoons as it can be hazardous and you may experience a landslide or two. Shillong, the capital, is a piece of colonial rule which got left behind by the British and it has Polo Grounds and a Golf Course which are frequented by many tourists.

Meghalaya has the largest number of caves in India and a visit to its ancient root bridges is a must do when you are visiting here.

Mizoram's landscape is something to be awed. With mountains, rivers, and gorges, no drive can be classified as safe because of its narrow roads and bridges.

The Chapchar Kut Festival is extremely popular and tourist flock to the state to attend it.

Tripura is known for its handloom and bamboo industry and here is where you can buy souvenirs from. The attraction here is Neermahal which was constructed as a summer resort for the Royals, and it is a must see when you visit.

WEST BENGAL

(Credit: mapsopensource.com & emapsworld.com)

This is one state that's not to be overlooked. From the fertile foothills of the Himalayas to the mangroves of the Bay of Bengal, this is without a doubt a land of remarkable contrasts. There is an amazing range of experiences all packed in a single state. West Bengal is also the fourth most populous states in India.

It borders Bangladesh in the east and Nepal and Bhutan in the north and therefore, it goes without saying that the scenery is some of the most beautiful you will see. From mountains to lakes, there's nothing these states don't have. In ancient times, it was Emperor Ashoka's territory but then colonized by the Gupta Empire. When it was colonized by the British, it was one of the few states which was open to change and people like Rabindranath Tagore the famous Noble prize winner poet are from Bengal.

In the south where the tropical climate is found, the village of Mandarmani is just as exciting and enchanting as the Bishnupur's Hindu temples and palaces. And for those of you who have been wondering, yes, you can find Bengal tigers in this area. They roam throughout the state, but if you visit Sunderbans, you find them swimming through the muddy rivers.

And your visit to West Bengal would not be complete without the European ghost towns lining the banks of the Hooghly River, one of the branches of the Ganges River.

It's also where you'll discover the "toy train" that through the train station of Darjeeling on its way to the town of Kurseong. If you've never heard of it, you must take this breathtaking trip. What makes this train so special? The amazing views you'll get from Khangchendong.

If you're an art-lover at heart or a foodie, this state also has a lively art scene and delicious cuisine.

WHERE TO GO

Singalila Ridge Trek provides you with a breathtaking 360-degree view of the mountains. Whether you're walking the ridgeline or admiring the scenery over a fresh, hot cup of tea, you'll discover why this is a once-in-a-lifetime opportunity.

Remember those terracotta temples mentioned in the previous paragraph? You'll find them tucked discretely into the city of Bishnupur. Probably one of the most beautiful is the pyramid-shaped Rasmancha, dating from approximately 1600.

But no trip to Bishnupur is complete without a visit to Jor Bangla Temple and its ornate carvings. And be sure to include the Madan Mohan Temple that's decorated with scenes from Hindu legends. If you visit the town proper, make a point to see the Bishnupur Museum, whet home of a myriad of ancient manuscripts and sculptures.

We've mentioned the Sundarbans Tiger Reserve. Visiting this is one of the best ways to boost the odds of spotting a Bengal tiger, but if you're determined to get that once-in-a-lifetime photo of a tiger, then you must include time at the Sundarbans Tiger Camp.

It's a guide through the reserve coupled with quality overnight accommodations in huts (yes, huts!) and quaint redbrick cottages that include forest-themed murals.

One last special recommendation on a must-see sight, especially if you're a history buff. That Sagar Island. Legend has it that it's here at the confluence of the Ganges, was the sight where King Sagar's 60,000 sons were resurrected by the flowing river after they had been reduced to ashes by the sage Kapil Muni.

Every January, the Ganga Saga Mela occurs not far from the Kapil Muni Temple, which honors this legend. You're encouraged to try if possible at all is by taking a one-night two-day, boat tour operated out of Kolkata by the West Bengal Tourism Center.

WHEN TO GO

Many wonder about the best time of the year to visit West Bengal. There are several answers to that, including there's no wrong time of the year. The other answer is that it depends on what you want to see and do.

There's something worth visiting just about every month of the year. Go in January if you want to wander through the mangrove forest of the Sundarbans Tiger Reserve.

If your passion is hiking, then you'll want to visit in either the spring – from March through May – with the flowers fresh in bloom or in the fall from October through December. Some individuals who have been there in the various seasons highly recommend October for the beautiful scenery.

If you plan on going any time during October through March, though, you'll want to avoid the heat on the lower southern plains.

Kolkata (Calcutta)

(Temple in Kolkata)

Kolkata is India's second largest city is a city of contrasts and contradictions. It's been called an ongoing "festival" of humankind, both luxurious and squalid, slow-moving and refine while at the same time frantically busy. And, in its own unique way, it's futuristic.

The capital city of West Bengal should be a stop on everyone's list of must-visit locations. Not only is Kolkata the political capital but it's also considered the artistic, cultural and intellectual capital of the entire country.

It's a natural "walking" city, much easier to get around on foot than any other way, despite the taxis and both motorized and human rickshaws.

Whether you're admiring the burgeoning art scene to experiencing the foodie's dream city, the moment you enter if you find yourself surrounded by bazaars. Ironically, just steps away from this you can find yourself sitting idly along the banks of the Hooghly River reveling in the sunset. Whatever your mood is, whatever your taste is, you'll find it in this remarkable city.

Amazingly, Kolkata also offers something for the book lover in you. It's host to the biggest book convention every year. Looking for a new book, or old, an ancient edition or those on the current best sellers list it's another must-see the sight of the city.

WHERE TO GO

For many, you say Kolkata and people immediately think of Mother Teresa, now St. Teresa. To this day, people visit the city for the sole purpose of making a pilgrimage to the Mother House, where she lived for some 50 years, her home base as she spent her lifetime feeding and caring for the poor of the city. Mother Teresa lies in rest there, and many come searching for a miracle healing.

Visit Kumartuli, a unique neighborhood where you can watch sculptors mold clay goddesses and coax them to life. After that, you may want to see the Belur Math, which has been called an "awe-inspiring." It's home-based to the worldwide, non-political and non-sectarian spiritual organizations Ramakrishna Math and Ramakrishna Mission. These organizations are more than a century old and have been involved in many humanitarian and social service activities within that time.

When you need a break from all the sights and sounds of the city, visit Millennium Park, a waterfront park. Here you can enjoy any number of boat rides as well as cruises. Close by is Millennium Park, which is a beautified waterfront park from where you can avail boat rides and cruises.

Once the sun goes down, you'll want to be along Park Street, a stretch of the street known for pubs and other clubs.

A Foodie's Heaven

The street food Kolkata is known through the entire country. Among your initial impressions of the city will be the abundance of eateries and food stalls wherever you turn. Choose from the local Bengali full meals or sample the region's famous snacks, like Jhal Muri, a spicy puffed rice treat or Ghugni Chaat, a simple dish that Bengalis eat in some form with all three meals of the day.

What's the Best Time to see Kolkata

Let's start off with what time of year you should avoid in this city. It's guaranteed you won't be able to get the best tastes, sounds and the sights of the Kolkata if you visit from May through September. It's definitely not for the lack of sights to see but simply because of the weather. The heavy rains of the season are certain to dampen your enjoyment.

But you may want to consider visiting in September, after the rains, and into October, if for no other reason than the Durga Puja. This is the festival that celebrates the Mother Goddess, Durga. Specifically, it celebrates her victory against Mahishasura, the evil buffalo demon. Metaphysically it honors the shakti or the universal female force.

If you're a film and music lover, then you'll want to plan your trip to the city in November through January. The weather, cool and dry, is a perfect backdrop to the myriad of film and music festivals throughout the city.

DARJEELING

(Credit: touristsinindia.blogspot.com)

From one look at West Bengal through the lens of the cacophony of sights, sounds, and tastes of Kolkata, we move to a once sleepy village of Darjeeling. Located in the northeastern region of India, this small town almost neighbors Nepal and Tibet.

Nestled in the rolling hills of the Himalayan Mountains, this town is peaceful and a stark contrast to the capital city of the state. The most notable aspect of this beautiful town is its worldwide reputation for growing tea.

Where to Go & What to Do

Darjeeling Himalayan Railway: The Toy Train

We've talked about the Toy Train briefly when we were describing West Bengal, we must mention it again. This is the town you can jump on it and take the round trip to Ghum and back.

It's called the Toy Train because this steam-powered train runs on a narrow-gauge track. Nicknamed, the "joy ride," you'll be inspired by the scenery and understand why that's an appropriate name.

Tiger Hill

This is a classic sight of Darjeeling, but the catch is that you need to visit it at sunrise. Even if you're not a morning person, you'll be so glad you made an effort to see the sun rise over the snow-covered Himalayan Mountains. There are taxis that will take you there, but some of them leave as early as 4 am, and you'll possibly find yourself sharing a ride with strangers. Yes, the cab drivers may wait until his vehicle is full until he leaves for the hill. So, you really do want to get an early start.

Happy Valley Tea Estate

What would a trip to Darjeeling famous for its tea production be without a trip to see the process in action? Rolling hills covered with tea plants seem to extend forever. There's no better place to tour than the Happy Valley Tea Estate.

Where to Eat

Singalila Restaurant

No trip to Darjeeling would be complete without at least one meal from the Singalila. Almost to a person, everyone who visits the city and eats here walks out feeling full – and wondering why food doesn't taste that good everywhere.

The establishment serves a combination of Nepali and Sikkimese food, many have called it the epitome of comfort food.

Hasty Tasty

Its location makes the Hasty Tasty restaurant an inevitable visit. While the food isn't quite up to Singalila, it does have "tasty" foods. Serving vegetarian, and Indian as well as Chinese food that will indeed entice you to eat there over and over again.

Kalden Café and Restaurant

This eatery specializes in Tibetan "fast" food, including momo dumplings, fried chow mein noodles, curry, and rice.

Glenary's Bakery

Not only does this bakery serve a wide assortment of baked goods and pastry, but Glenary's also serves a wide array of sandwiches. One of the advantages of this establishment is that it opens early.

WHEN TO GO

There are two best times of the year to visit this relaxing, beautiful town. You'll want to choose March to May, that's spring and summer, and then the between the months of October and November. These latter months are considered autumn.

When the June weather rolls around, you may not want to be here. This month starts the monsoon season and lasts until September. If you're unfamiliar with this "season," it brings torrents of rain.

CONCLUSION

India is a versatile country with much to see. As I mentioned earlier, it is impossible to touch on all the destinations it has to offer and the beauty of the country. If you do plan to visit India, it is good to do so in winter as the summer is extremely hot and bothersome.

Getting around is easy as one can take flights from major cities and cars are easily available for hire at local tourist companies. It is, however, better to fly from one place to another as the roads can be awful and bumpy. For day trips, there may not be an option, but many of the highways are good but the travel time can range from 2 hours to 8 hours and can get very tiring.

It is important to keep in mind that Indians can be conservative and if you do something to offend them, they are not likely to be nice. People can also be over friendly, and that is something you should be careful of as they can be pickpockets, so you need to take care of your belongings and keep them safe at all times.

Although Indians are more than happy to help foreigners, one must keep in mind that not all must be befriended and sometimes as bad as it sounds, people may follow you, and that can't be good.

Another useful tip which might help is that keeping small change with you at all times can be good as many people will argue and pocket the big notes if you do not have it saying they do not have the money to pay you back.

Bargaining is another thing which you can brush up on before visiting as many of the street vendors will quote a much higher price for souvenirs, and you need to try and get them down a notch. People will argue that the artifacts are original, but a quality check is imperative in order to ensure that.

If you are traveling alone as a woman, it is better to go through a guided tour company especially in North India. Of course, there will be more do's and don'ts, but I guess this is about it. All I can say now is see you all in India!

Namaste!

(Credit: Wikispacs.com)

Printed by Amazon Italia Logistica S.r.l.
Torrazza Piemonte (TO), Italy